UNDERSTANDING THE FIVE ELEMENTS

A GUIDE TO HINDU COSMOLOGY AND TRADITION

DR. JAGADEESH PILLAI

Made with ♥ on the Notion Press Platform
www.notionpress.com

|| Dedicated to All Wisdom Seekers Around The World ||

Contents

Prayer *vii*

About The Author *ix*

Preface *xiii*

1. Five Elements Or Pancha-tatwa 1

Part 1

2. Pancha-tatwa Treatment 7

Part 2

3. The Pancha Tatwa In The Vedas 13

Part 3

4. The Five Elements In The Upanishads 17

Part 4

5. The Pancha Tatwa In The Puranas 21

Part 5

6. The Five Elements And The Human Body 25

Part 6

7. The Five Elements And Yoga 29

Part 7

8. The Five Elements And Ayurveda 33

Part 8

9. Five Elements And Chakras 39

Part 9

10. Five Elements And Astrology 45

Part 10

11. The Five Elements And The Hindu Calendar 51

Contents

Part 11

12. The Five Elements And Hindu Temple Architecture 57

Part 12

13. The Pancha Tatwa In Hindu Art And Literature 61

Part 13

14. The Five Elements And Hindu Environmentalism 65

Part 14

15. The Pancha Tatwa And The Gunas 69

Part 15

16. Begin And End With Pacha-tatwa 73

Other Books Of The Author 75

Contact 79

Prayer

"Om Bhadram Karnebhih Shrunuyaama DevaahBhadram Pashyemaakshabhiryajatraah SthirairangaistushtuvaamsastanoobhihVyashema Devahitam YadaayuhSwasti Na Indro VridhashravaahSwasti Nah Pooshaa VishwavedaahSwasti Nastaarkshyo ArishtanemihSwasti No Brihaspatir DadhaatuOm Shantih, Shantih, Shantih"

The literal meaning of this mantra is: OM. O Gods! Let us hear auspicious words from our ears. O reverent Gods! Let us behold propitious visions from our eyes, let our organs and body be stable, healthy, and strong. Let us do that which is pleasing to the gods in the life span allotted to us. May Indra, inscribed in the scriptures, bring us fortune! May Pushan, the knower of the world, grant us prosperity! May Trakshya, who vanquishes enemies, bestow us with blessings! May Brihaspati bring us success!
OM Peace, Peace, Peace.

About The Author

Dr. Jagadeesh Pillai is a renowned Guinness World Record holder, writer, and researcher hailing from Varanasi, also known as the abode of Lord Shiva. With a Ph.D. in Vedic Science and a range of creative ideas and achievements, he is a true polymath. He is the author of more than 100 books including Research Publications. Although his roots can be traced back to Kerala, the people of Varanasi hold him in high regard and affectionately consider him one of their own.

Dr. Pillai has achieved four Guinness World Records in the following subjects:

1. "Script to Screen" - In this record, Dr. Pillai produced and directed an animation film within the shortest time possible, breaking the previous record set by Canadians. He has also received numerous national and international awards and recognitions for this achievement.

2. Longest Line of Postcards - For this record, Dr. Pillai created a line of 16,300 postcards on the occasion of the 163rd anniversary of Indian Postal Day. The event also included a questionnaire about the Indian flag.

3. Largest Poster Awareness Campaign - Dr. Pillai designed an awareness campaign on the subject of "Beti Bachao - Beti Padhao" (Save the Girl Child - Educate the Girl Child)

to achieve this record.

4. Largest Envelope - In tribute to the Indian Prime Minister's "Make in India" initiative, Dr. Pillai created a 4000 square meter envelope using waste paper to achieve this record.

5. Attempted - 70000 Candles on a 210 kg Cake - To celebrate the 70th Indian Independence Day, Dr. Pillai attempted to light 70,000 candles on a 210 kg cake, which was recorded in World Records India.

6. Attempted - Documentary on Dhamek Stupa of Sarnath in 17 Languages - Dr. Pillai attempted to create a documentary on the Dhamek Stupa of Sarnath, dubbing it in 17 different languages. The result of this attempt is currently awaiting confirmation from the Guinness World Records.

Dr. Pillai is skilled in teaching the Bhagavad Gita, a Hindu scripture, and is popular among young people. He has helped many young people improve their lives through his motivational teachings.

In addition to teaching, he has composed and sung numerous Sanskrit Bhajans and patriotic songs.

He has also written and directed several short films and documentaries for awareness campaigns, and has volunteered with the police in both UP and Kerala to spread awareness about various issues through videos and photography.

He has a goal of writing thousands of books on Indian culture, Indian temples, and the lives of extraordinary people. Incredibly, he has produced and directed over 100 documentaries about the city of Varanasi, all on his own.

He has also helped and guided more than 25 boys and girls to achieve world records through creative and innovative methods. He is a multifaceted person who uses his intellect and the blessings given to him by God to excel in various areas. He is both a teacher and a student, always learning and teaching, and is able to master any subject he comes across.

He is a selfless social activist and motivational speaker who has overcome struggles and failures to become a successful and enthusiastic individual with a rich life experience.

In addition to his work with the Bhagavad Gita, he is also an efficient Tarot card reader, Astro-Vastu consultant, and a talented singer and composer. He has sung the entire Ram Charita Manas and Bhagavad Gita in his own compositions, and has sung the phrase "Lokah Samastha Sukhino Bhavantu" in 50 different languages. He is currently working on a detailed and scientific study of Vedas, Upanishads, Puranas, and the Bhagavad Gita. He has also composed and sung the Hanuman Chalisa and Gayatri Mantra in 108 and 1008 different compositions, respectively.

Awards - Four Times Guinness World Records, Winner of

Mahatma Gandhi Vishwa Shanti Puraskar , Mahatma Gandhi Global Peace Ambassador, Kashi Ratna Award, Dr. APJ Abdul Kalam Motivational Person of the Year 2017, Mother Teresa Award, Indira Gandhi Priyadarshini Award, Bharat Vikas Ratna Award, Udyog Ratna Award, Vigyan Prasar Award, Poorvanchal Ratn Samman.

PREFACE

In the ancient Hindu scriptures, the Pancha Tatwa, or Five Elements, are revered as the fundamental building blocks of the universe. These elements - earth, water, fire, air, and space - are believed to encompass all of creation, from the smallest particle to the vast expanse of the cosmos. In Hindu tradition, the Pancha Tatwa are more than just physical substances - they are also powerful forces that shape our world and our lives.

In this book, we delve into the rich history and symbolism of the Pancha Tatwa, exploring their role in Hindu scriptures such as the Vedas, Upanishads, and Puranas. We examine the ways in which the Five Elements are woven into the fabric of Hindu rituals and practices, and how they are connected to the natural world, the human body, and the cosmos. We also explore the influence of the Pancha Tatwa on Hindu philosophy, mythology, and art, and how they continue to shape contemporary Hindu thought and practice.

Whether you are new to Hinduism or an experienced student of this rich and ancient tradition, this book offers a fascinating journey of discovery into the world of the Pancha Tatwa. Through its pages, you will come to understand the profound significance of these Five Elements, and how they continue to shape the world we live in today.

I

Five Elements or Pancha-Tatwa

It is believed in Sankhya Shastra that this nature is made up of five elements| Panchtattva is also known as Panchamahabhuta or Panchabhuta and is considered to be the core of Indian philosophy| Every substance in the universe is made up of five elements, but the substances made of the five elements are inanimate, so they need a soul to become living| The Panchtattva is described in the 'Ashta Khand' of "Jabaldarshanopanishad" associated with samaveda and this Panchtattva is as follows:

1 – Sky (Space)

2 – Air (Quark)

3 – Agni (Energy)

4 – Water (Force)

5 – Earth (Matter)

It is believed in yoga that the food body is also made up of these five elements. Our soul is made up of five elements sky, air, fire, water and earth, but have you ever wondered in which part of our body these five elements are there? What is its size? What is its color? What does it work for? Is there a mantra? What is its quality? It is associated with which cycle? Many questions.

These five elements are so important and mysterious that it is not possible to explain in detail, but here an attempt is being made to explain some important facts as far as possible. By dividing our body into five parts, let's try to understand the effects of these five elements:

1 – Sky Element (Space)

The area of our head, i.e., the area above our eyebrows, is said to be a part of the sky element and this element is circal. Sadashiv should be considered in this part of this sky element. This element is related to the sixteen-petaled blue chakra, whose **"HAM"** is the seed mantra. Earth, water, fire and air are present in the sky element. These sky elements are considered to be the carriers of our soul and it requires spiritual practice to experience it. The element of sky is called the mind immaterially because just as the sky is infinite, so the mind is also infinite. This mind is present inside our body in the form of sky element, just as the sky is sometimes completely calm and sometimes surrounded by badlo, similarly the mind is also troubled by thoughts. Sometimes it's quiet.

2 – Air (Quark)

From our heart to the middle of the eyebrows above, the fraction of air is fixed and it is hexagonal. One should think of God in this part of the air element. This element is related to the twelve-petaled Anahat Chakra of green color, whose **"YAM"** is the beej mantra. The origin of fire by air is believed to be. Our prana is considered to be the air element, if the air element goes out of the body, then our prana will also be removed. This air is our age because we are alive only from the air we breathe i.e. oxygen.

3 – Agni (Energy)

The area from our anus to the heart region is called a part of the fire element and this element is triangular. Mahadevji should be considered in part of this fire element. This element is related to the yellow-colored manipura chakra with ten petals, whose **"RAM"** is the beej mantra. Water is believed to have originated by fire. The element of fire digests food and keeps our body healthy and provides strength and strength. This fire element is present in the form of energy in us and whatever warmth is in our body is due to the fire element.

4 – Water (Force)

Our knee to anus is said to be a part of the water element and this element is crescentic. Vishnu should be considered in this part of this water element. This element is related to the six-petaled sacral chakra of orange color, whose **"VAM"** is the beej mantra. Water is considered to be the origin of the root world. Just as 70% water is found on earth, similarly about 70% water is found in our body. Whatever fluids flowing in our body and on the earth are called water elements such as water, blood, fat, enzymes and many types of juices made in the body, etc.

5 – Earth (Matter)

The area from our foot to the knee is said to be a fraction of the earth element and this element is rectangle. One should think of Brahma ji in this part of this earth element. This element is related to the root chakra with four petals of red color, whose **"LAM"** is the seed mantra. The earth is called part or part of the root world. The elements, metals and non-metals from which the earth is made (also for the soil) is made of our body.

There is also an element above the above five elements which we call atma i.e. Om and due to this soul, these five elements are able to do their work. Therefore, at the time of conception of each element, the mantras Ham, Yam, Ram, Vam, Lam Beej mantras should be chanted respectively. This notion is described as the best and is an act of destruction of sins. If we want to live a long life healthy, then we should understand its importance and respect it.

“To forget how to dig the earth and to tend the soil is to forget ourselves.”

— Mahatma Gandhi

II

Pancha-Tatwa Treatment

If we have to live our life happily and peacefully, then first of all we have to live according to nature, otherwise it is normal to have diseases in the body. Our body remains healthy only by the result and order of the five elements of nature, but if there is a disturbance in their result and order, then we start to remain unwell. When we know that a disease is caused by a deficiency or excess of such an element, then that element can be prevented by use.

Soil Element:

In ancient times, sage sages often used to make raw huts or cottage caves by digging themselves, etc., due to which their health was strong and fully nourished. They used to achieve longevity only through diet. Small children who play in dust and soil are believed to have physical growth very quickly and injuries heal more quickly because the soil has amazing power to pull disorders.

Water Element:

Many disorders within the body come out in the form of sweat and urine with water and using the right amount of water helps in strengthening physical health. Because there are many chemical elements in water that provide adequate nutrition to our body, regular bathing, Kartik bath, Magh bath, pilgrimage bath, festival bath, etc. have been reported in our country since ancient times, it is said that the people of Europe did not bathe much due to cold, but when they came to know the important facts of bathing with water, they started bathing.

Element of Fire:

First of all, agni mel purohitam is said to be important among all the elements. The sun is the symbol of fire or the fire is the representative of the sun. If the fire element in the body is eliminated, then life will also end. Western scientists have also accepted that they have brought a new system of medicine for prevention of diseases through the sun's rays. In many hospitals there, treatment is being done only by sun rays. Hundreds of impossible diseases are being cured by separating the ultraviolet rays of the sun by machines. Seven types of colored glass and water filled in bottles are also being used to prevent disease and it is also believed that the sun's rays have the highest potential to destroy the germs of the disease.

Elements of air:

The subtle element of the five elements is air and air is considered to be prana. Without food and water, humans can survive for some time or a few days, but not without air. If someone has to be unconscious, he will faint as soon as he smells the sedation medicine, but eating will not come so soon. Therefore, due to this quality, the sages invented the effective method of yajna-havan. Through havan, the air element and the brain maintain health.

Many scientists have described how the medicines used in havana take a subtle form together in marriage and affect our body:

Tizvert: - The test of French scientist Professor Tizvert has proved that diseases like cholera, tuberculosis, TV, smallpox, etc. can be destroyed by the gas produced by the burning of sugar, food.

Dr. Haffkine, the inventor of the ticket for the French scientist plague, has told that the gas released by the burning of cow's ghee. It can destroy skin diseases, blood disorders, dryness, inflammation and intestinal disease disorders.

Dr. Tatlik said that typhoid and pneumonia can be treated by the gas produced in the smoke.

Dr. M. Trails said that the gas emitted by burning fruits like munakka raisins etc. destroys typhoid germs.

Sky Elements:

The element of sky cannot be experienced, but one must be

introduced to the working form because this element is the most subtle. This element occurs in every pole space and scientists call it "ether". (Ether is an organic compound that two alkyl molecules are attached to the same oxygen. ***(the common formula is R-O R).***

Whatever we hear reaches us only through the sky element, otherwise we cannot hear anything like baja, bell, car, etc. The sky element cannot be separated in any way. Because this fact maintains the existence of matter by being present in every place.

Note : *(General Formula* **ROR** *is - In organic chemistry, ethers are a class of compounds that contain an ether group—an oxygen atom connected to two alkyl or aryl groups. They have the general formula R–O–R′, where R and R′ represent the alkyl or aryl groups)*

"Touching the earth – digging, planting, harvesting – connects us literally and spiritually to those who have dug, planted and harvested before us."

— Peg Streep

ꙮ

III

The Pancha Tatwa in the Vedas

The Pancha Tatwa, or Five Elements, are a central concept in Hinduism and are revered as the fundamental building blocks of the universe. These elements - earth, water, fire, air, and space - are believed to encompass all of creation, from the smallest particle to the vast expanse of the cosmos. In the Vedas, the oldest and most sacred texts of Hinduism, the Pancha Tatwa are described as the foundation of the material world and the source of all life.

In the Vedas, the Pancha Tatwa are described as the five primary energies of the universe. Each element is associated with a specific quality and function, and is believed to be present in all things. Earth is associated with solidity and stability, water with fluidity and nourishment, fire with heat and transformation, air with movement and communication, and space with expansion and infinite potential.

The Pancha Tatwa are also believed to be intimately connected to the human body. In Hindu tradition, the elements are thought to be present in the body in the form of the three doshas - Vata, Pitta, and Kapha - which govern different bodily functions and characteristics. Imbalances in the doshas are thought to be the root cause of many physical and mental health issues, and maintaining balance between the elements is seen as key to maintaining overall well-being.

In addition to their physical and physiological roles, the Pancha Tatwa also have a spiritual significance in Hinduism. In the Vedas, the elements are seen as the means through which the individual soul, or Atman, can achieve union with the ultimate reality, or Brahman. The elements are believed to be the vehicles through which the Atman can transcend the material world and experience the ultimate unity and oneness of the universe.

The Pancha Tatwa play a central role in the Vedas and in Hinduism more broadly. They are seen as the fundamental building blocks of the universe and the source of all life, and are intimately connected to the human body and the spiritual journey of the individual soul. Understanding the Pancha Tatwa is essential to understanding the teachings and practices of Hinduism.

"The miracle is to walk on the green earth, dwelling deeply in the present moment and feeling truly alive."

— Thich Nhat Hanh

ᘓ

IV

The Five Elements in the Upanishads

The Five Elements, also known as the pancha mahabhutas, are a central concept in the Upanishads, ancient Hindu scriptures that contain some of the foundational ideas of Hinduism. These elements are earth, water, fire, air, and space, and they are believed to be the building blocks of the entire universe.

In the Upanishads, the Five Elements are seen as having both physical and metaphysical properties. On a physical level, they are the basic substances that make up the material world, and they are also thought to have certain qualities and characteristics. For example, earth is solid and stable, water is fluid and cleansing, fire is hot and transformative, air is light and mobile, and space is infinite and all-encompassing.

On a metaphysical level, the Five Elements are seen as

having a deeper significance, as they are believed to be connected to the essence of the universe and to the divine. Each element is associated with a particular aspect of reality, and they are seen as being interconnected and interdependent. For example, earth is connected to the body and the material world, water is connected to the emotions and the psyche, fire is connected to the intellect and the senses, air is connected to the breath and the life force, and space is connected to the soul and the ultimate reality.

In the Upanishads, the Five Elements are also seen as being linked to the different aspects of the self, and they are believed to be present within every individual. It is believed that by understanding and working with the elements within ourselves, we can gain a deeper understanding of the world around us and our place within it.

In conclusion, the Five Elements are a central concept in the Upanishads, and they are seen as having both physical and metaphysical properties. They are believed to be the building blocks of the universe and to be connected to the essence of reality and the divine. Understanding and working with the elements within ourselves is believed to be an important step in gaining a deeper understanding of the world and our place within it.

"You are a guest. Leave this earth a little more beautiful, a little more human, a little more lovable, a little more fragrant, for those unknown guests who will be following you."

— Osho

☙

V

The Pancha Tatwa in the Puranas

The Pancha Tatwa, also known as the Five Great Elements, are a central concept in the Puranas, a group of Hindu scriptures that contain myths, legends, and teachings about the religion. The Five Great Elements are earth, water, fire, air, and ether, and they are believed to be the building blocks of the entire universe.

In the Puranas, the Pancha Tatwa are seen as having both physical and metaphysical properties. On a physical level, they are the basic substances that make up the material world, and they are also thought to have certain qualities and characteristics. For example, earth is solid and stable, water is fluid and cleansing, fire is hot and transformative, air is light and mobile, and ether is all-encompassing and the source of all sound.

On a metaphysical level, the Pancha Tatwa are seen as

having a deeper significance, as they are believed to be connected to the essence of the universe and to the divine. Each element is associated with a particular aspect of reality, and they are seen as being interconnected and interdependent. For example, earth is connected to the body and the material world, water is connected to the emotions and the psyche, fire is connected to the intellect and the senses, air is connected to the breath and the life force, and ether is connected to the soul and the ultimate reality.

In the Puranas, the Pancha Tatwa are also seen as being linked to the different aspects of the self, and they are believed to be present within every individual. It is believed that by understanding and working with the elements within ourselves, we can gain a deeper understanding of the world around us and our place within it.

In conclusion, the Pancha Tatwa are a central concept in the Puranas, and they are seen as having both physical and metaphysical properties. They are believed to be the building blocks of the universe and to be connected to the essence of reality and the divine. Understanding and working with the elements within ourselves is believed to be an important step in gaining a deeper understanding of the world and our place within it.

"All know that the drop merges into the ocean but few know that the ocean merges into the drop."

— Kabir

ꕤ

VI

The Five Elements and the Human Body

In Hindu philosophy, the Five Elements (also known as the pancha mahabhutas or the Pancha Tatwa) are believed to be present within the human body and to be connected to various physical and metaphysical aspects of the self. Each element is associated with a particular aspect of the body and is thought to have certain qualities and characteristics.

Here is a brief overview of the Five Elements and their association with the human body:

Earth: This element is associated with the solid structure of the body, including the bones, skin, and tissues. It is also connected to the sense of smell and the feeling of being grounded and stable.

Water: This element is associated with the fluids of the body, including blood, saliva, and mucus. It is also connected to the sense of taste and the feeling of emotion and flow.

Fire: This element is associated with the body's metabolism and digestion, as well as the senses of sight and touch. It is also connected to the feeling of heat and transformation.

Air: This element is associated with the movement of the body, including breathing, circulation, and the sense of touch. It is also connected to the feeling of lightness and mobility.

Space: This element is associated with the body's cavities and the sense of hearing. It is also connected to the feeling of expansion and infinite possibility.

It is important to note that the Five Elements are not limited to specific locations within the body, but rather, they are thought to be present throughout the body and to be interconnected and interdependent. In Hindu philosophy, understanding and working with the elements within ourselves is believed to be an important step in gaining a deeper understanding of the self and our place in the world.

"You can't stop the waves, but you can learn to surf."

— Jon Kabat-Zinn

VII

The Five Elements and Yoga

In Hindu philosophy, the Five Elements (also known as the pancha mahabhutas or the Pancha Tatwa) are believed to be present within the human body and to be connected to various physical and metaphysical aspects of the self. In yoga, the Five Elements are often associated with different yoga poses (asanas) and are thought to have specific benefits for the body and mind.

Here is a brief overview of how the Five Elements are connected to yoga and the benefits they are thought to provide:

Earth: This element is associated with yoga poses that involve stability and grounding, such as mountain pose (tadasana) and tree pose (vrksasana). These poses are believed to help improve balance and stability, as well as to cultivate a sense of calm and centeredness.

Water: This element is associated with yoga poses that involve fluid movement, such as cat-cow pose (marjaryasana-bitilasana) and downward-facing dog (adho mukha svanasana). These poses are believed to help improve flexibility and circulation, as well as to reduce stress and tension.

Fire: This element is associated with yoga poses that involve heat and intensity, such as sun salutations (surya namaskar) and warrior poses (virabhadrasana). These poses are believed to help improve strength and stamina, as well as to increase focus and determination.

Air: This element is associated with yoga poses that involve movement and breath, such as alternate nostril breathing (nadi shodhana) and eagle pose (garudasana). These poses are believed to help improve respiratory function and increase energy, as well as to improve balance and coordination.

Space: This element is associated with yoga poses that involve openness and expansion, such as seated forward bend (paschimottanasana) and child's pose (balasana). These poses are believed to help improve flexibility and relaxation, as well as to cultivate a sense of peace and calm.

Overall, the Five Elements are an important concept in yoga, and incorporating poses that correspond to each element can help to balance and harmonize the body and mind.

"The river that flows in you also flows in me."

— Kabir

ഇ

VIII

The Five Elements and Ayurveda

In Ayurveda, an ancient system of medicine that originated in India, the Five Elements (also known as the pancha mahabhutas) are believed to be the building blocks of the universe and to be present within the human body. These elements are earth, water, fire, air, and space, and they are thought to have specific qualities and characteristics that influence the functioning of the body and the mind.

In Ayurveda, each element is associated with a particular type of tissue (dhatu) and with a specific body type (dosha). The elements are also believed to be connected to certain emotions, behaviors, and physical characteristics. Here is a brief overview of the Five Elements and their association with Ayurveda:

Earth: This element is associated with the solid tissues of the body, such as the bones and muscles, and with the

Kapha dosha. Earth is thought to be heavy, stable, and grounding, and it is believed to be associated with qualities such as stability, endurance, and calmness. In Ayurveda, imbalances in the earth element can manifest as sluggishness, excess weight, and congestion. Treatment for earth element imbalances may include therapies such as herbal remedies, dietary changes, and physical exercise.

Water: This element is associated with the fluid tissues of the body, such as the blood and lymph, and with the Kapha dosha. Water is thought to be fluid, moist, and cooling, and it is believed to be associated with qualities such as flow, lubrication, and emotionality. In Ayurveda, imbalances in the water element can manifest as edema, congestion, and excess mucus. Treatment for water element imbalances may include therapies such as herbal remedies, warm oils, and steam therapy.

Fire: This element is associated with the metabolic tissues of the body, such as the blood and skin, and with the Pitta dosha. Fire is thought to be hot, sharp, and transformative, and it is believed to be associated with qualities such as intellect, digestion, and passion. In Ayurveda, imbalances in the fire element can manifest as inflammation, excess acidity, and irritation. Treatment for fire element imbalances may include therapies such as herbal remedies, cooling oils, and meditation.

Air: This element is associated with the movement tissues of the body, such as the muscles and nerves, and with the Vata dosha. Air is thought to be light, mobile, and dry, and it is believed to be associated with qualities such as creativity, communication, and flexibility. In Ayurveda, imbalances in the air element can manifest as dryness, anxiety, and irregularity. Treatment for air element imbalances may include therapies such as herbal remedies, warm oils, and yoga.

Space: This element is associated with the cavities of the body, such as the sinuses and joints, and with the Vata dosha. Space is thought to be expansive, infinite, and all-encompassing, and it is believed to be associated with qualities such as openness, receptivity, and communication. In Ayurveda, imbalances in the space element can manifest as emptiness, insecurity, and instability. Treatment for space element imbalances may include therapies such as herbal remedies, warm oils, and meditation.

Overall, the Five Elements are an important concept in Ayurveda, and understanding their influence on the body and mind can help to identify imbalances and choose appropriate treatments.

"The stream of life is a wave on the ocean of love."

— Maharishi Mahesh Yogi

IX

Five Elements and Chakras

In Hindu philosophy, the Five Elements (also known as the pancha mahabhutas or the Pancha Tatwa) are believed to be present within the human body and to be connected to various physical and metaphysical aspects of the self. These elements are earth, water, fire, air, and space, and they are thought to have specific qualities and characteristics that influence the functioning of the body and the mind.

The Five Elements are also connected to the chakras, which are energy centers located within the body. According to Hindu belief, there are seven main chakras, and each chakra is associated with a particular element, as well as with a specific color, beej mantra (sacred sound), and set of physical and psychological functions. Here is a brief overview of the connection between the Five Elements and the chakras:

Earth: The root chakra (muladhara) is associated with the element of earth and is located at the base of the spine. It is associated with the color red, the beej mantra "LAM," and the physical and psychological functions of stability, security, and grounding. Imbalances in the root chakra can manifest as issues with the feet, legs, and lower back, as well as with feelings of fear, insecurity, and lack of purpose. To help balance the root chakra, one can practice grounding and stability-enhancing yoga poses, use the color red and the beej mantra "LAM," and focus on feelings of safety and security.

Water: The sacral chakra (svadhishthana) is associated with the element of water and is located in the lower abdomen. It is associated with the color orange, the beej mantra "VAM," and the physical and psychological functions of sexuality, creativity, and emotions. Imbalances in the sacral chakra can manifest as issues with the reproductive system, urinary system, and lower back, as well as with feelings of guilt, shame, and lack of creativity. To help balance the sacral chakra, one can practice fluid and creative yoga poses, use the color orange and the beej mantra "VAM," and focus on feelings of pleasure and creativity.

Fire: The solar plexus chakra (manipura) is associated with the element of fire and is located in the upper abdomen. It is associated with the color yellow, the beej mantra "RAM," and the physical and psychological functions of digestion, metabolism, and personal power. Imbalances in the solar plexus chakra can manifest as issues with the digestive system, liver, and pancreas, as well as with feelings of insecurity, low self-esteem, and anger. To help balance the solar plexus chakra, one can practice heat-building yoga poses, use the color yellow and the beej mantra "RAM," and focus on feelings of self-worth and personal power.

Air: The heart chakra (anahata) is associated with the element of air and is located in the center of the chest. It is associated with the color green, the beej mantra "YAM," and the physical and psychological functions of love, compassion, and connection. Imbalances in the heart chakra can manifest as issues with the heart, lungs, and upper back, as well as with feelings of grief, loneliness, and lack of love. To help balance the heart chakra, one can practice expansive and open yoga poses, use the color green and the beej mantra "YAM," and focus on feelings of love and compassion.

Space, also known as akasha in Sanskrit, is the element associated with the crown chakra, located at the top of the head. The color associated with this element is violet or white, and the beej mantra is "Om". This element represents spiritual connection and higher consciousness. When the crown chakra is balanced, one may feel a sense of unity with the universe and a connection to their higher self. Imbalances in the crown chakra can manifest as disconnection from one's spirituality or a lack of purpose. To help balance this chakra, one can meditate on the beej mantra, visualize the color violet or white, or practice yoga poses that focus on the crown chakra such as headstands or shoulderstands. Overall, the element of space is an important aspect of one's spiritual and personal growth, and promoting balance in the crown chakra can lead to a greater sense of inner peace and understanding.

"Set your life on fire, seek those who fan your flames."

— Rumi

☙❧

X

Five Elements and Astrology

The Pancha Tatwa, also known as the five elements, are a fundamental concept in Hindu astrology and philosophy. These elements are earth, water, fire, air, and space, and they are believed to make up the entire universe and all living beings within it. Each element is associated with a specific planet and nakshatra (lunar mansion), and understanding the relationship between these elements can provide insight into an individual's personality and life path.

The element of earth is associated with the planet Saturn and the nakshatra Rohini. This element represents stability, structure, and material possessions. Those with a strong earth element may be practical, reliable, and grounded, but an imbalance in this element can lead to greed or attachment to material possessions.

The element of water is associated with the planet Venus and the nakshatra Bharani. This element represents emotions, creativity, and the ability to adapt. Those with a strong water element may be emotionally intelligent and able to go with the flow, but an imbalance in this element can lead to a lack of boundaries or emotional instability.

The element of fire is associated with the planet Mars and the nakshatra Krittika. This element represents passion, determination, and action. Those with a strong fire element may be ambitious and driven, but an imbalance in this element can lead to anger and aggression.

The element of air is associated with the planet Mercury and the nakshatra Mrigashira. This element represents communication, intelligence, and movement. Those with a strong air element may be intellectual and quick-witted, but an imbalance in this element can lead to a lack of focus or scattered energy.

The element of space is associated with the planet Jupiter and the nakshatra Mula. This element represents spiritual connection and higher consciousness. Those with a strong space element may be spiritually inclined and open-minded, but an imbalance in this element can lead to a disconnection from one's spirituality or a lack of purpose.

In Hindu astrology, the position and strength of these elements in an individual's birth chart can provide insight into their personality and life path. Understanding the Pancha Tatwa can also help individuals work towards balance within themselves and their lives. For example, if someone has an imbalance in the earth element, they may benefit from finding ways to let go of material possessions and focus on inner stability. On the other hand, someone with an imbalance in the water element may benefit from finding ways to strengthen their emotional intelligence and set boundaries.

Overall, the Pancha Tatwa and their connection to the planets and nakshatras play a significant role in Hindu astrology and can provide valuable insight into an individual's personality and path in life. By understanding and balancing these elements within ourselves, we can strive for harmony and personal growth.

"Of all fires, love is the only inexhaustible one."

— Pablo Neruda

ꟹ

XI

The Five Elements and the Hindu Calendar

The Five Elements, also known as the Pancha Tatwa, are a fundamental concept in Hindu philosophy and are believed to make up the entire universe and all living beings within it. These elements are earth, water, fire, air, and space. In Hinduism, these elements are also associated with the Hindu calendar and certain months and festivals.

The element of earth is associated with the months of October and November, which fall during the Hindu lunar month of Ashwin. This element represents stability, structure, and material possessions. During this time, many Hindus celebrate the festival of Navaratri, which honors the goddess Durga and symbolizes the victory of good over evil.

The element of water is associated with the months of

December and January, which fall during the Hindu lunar month of Margashirsha. This element represents emotions, creativity, and the ability to adapt.

The element of fire is associated with the months of February and March, which fall during the Hindu lunar month of Pausha. This element represents passion, determination, and action. During this time, many Hindus celebrate the festival of Holi, which marks the victory of good over evil and the arrival of spring.

The element of air is associated with the months of April and May, which fall during the Hindu lunar month of Magha. This element represents communication, intelligence, and movement. During this time, many Hindus celebrate the festival of Mahavir Jayanti, which commemorates the birth of Mahavira, the founder of Jainism.

The element of space is associated with the months of June and July, which fall during the Hindu lunar month of Phalguna. This element represents spiritual connection and higher consciousness. During this time, many Hindus celebrate the festival of Vaisakhi, which marks the start of the solar year and the harvest season.

In Hinduism, each element is believed to have a specific energy and influence on the world and on individual lives. Understanding the connection between the Five Elements and the Hindu calendar can provide insight into the energies and themes present during certain months and festivals. By aligning with these energies and incorporating them into our lives, we can strive for balance and harmony.

“The mind is not a vessel to be filled, but a fire to be kindled.”

— Plutarch

XII

The Five Elements and Hindu Temple Architecture

The Five Elements, also known as the Pancha Tatwa, are a fundamental concept in Hindu philosophy and are believed to make up the entire universe and all living beings within it. These elements are earth, water, fire, air, and space. In Hindu temple architecture, these elements are often represented and incorporated into the design and construction of the temple.

The element of earth is represented through the use of solid materials such as stone, brick, and wood in the construction of the temple. The temple's foundation, or garbhagriha, is often made of stone or brick and symbolizes the element of earth.

The element of water is represented through the use of

water features such as pools, fountains, and tanks within the temple complex. Water is also often used in Hindu rituals and ceremonies, and the presence of water features in a temple can facilitate these rituals.

The element of fire is represented through the use of a sacred fire, or agni, which is often present in the temple and is used in rituals and ceremonies. The agni is often symbolized by a lamp or other lighting feature in the temple.

The element of air is represented through the use of open spaces and the incorporation of natural elements such as trees and gardens within the temple complex. These elements allow for the circulation of fresh air and promote a sense of peace and tranquility within the temple.

The element of space is represented through the use of open, spacious areas within the temple complex, which allows for the expansion of consciousness and the opportunity for spiritual contemplation. The temple's main shrine, or garbhagriha, is often designed as an open, spacious area to symbolize the element of space.

In Hindu temple architecture, the incorporation of the Five Elements is believed to promote balance and harmony within the temple complex and to facilitate spiritual growth and connection for those who visit. Each element is believed to have a specific energy and influence, and the presence of all five elements within the temple helps to create a holistic, sacred space.

"You are pure space, uncontaminated by anything. You are just a mirror reflecting nothing."

— Osho

ꕤ

XIII

The Pancha Tatwa in Hindu Art and Literature

The Pancha Tatwa, or Five Elements, are a fundamental concept in Hindu art and literature. These elements, which are Earth, Water, Fire, Air, and Space, are seen as the basic building blocks of the universe and are believed to be present in all living and non-living things.

In Hindu art and literature, the Five Elements are often depicted and referenced in various forms of art, such as music, dance, and literature. In music, for example, each element is associated with a particular sound or musical quality. For instance, the element of Earth is associated with the lower pitches, while the element of Air is associated with higher pitches. In dance, the elements are often represented through the movements and gestures of the dancers. For example, the element of Fire might be represented through sharp, angular movements, while the element of Water might be represented through fluid, flowing movements.

The Five Elements are also often depicted in Hindu art and literature through the use of symbols and imagery. For example, the element of Earth might be represented through the use of earthy colors, such as brown and green, while the element of Fire might be represented through the use of bright, fiery colors, such as red and orange. In literature, the elements are often used as symbols or metaphors to convey deeper meaning and themes. For example, the element of Water might be used to symbolize emotion or change, while the element of Earth might be used to represent stability and solidity.

The Pancha Tatwa, or Five Elements, play a central role in Hindu art and literature. They are represented and referenced in various forms of art, such as music, dance, and literature, and are often used to convey deeper meaning and themes. By understanding and exploring the connection between the Five Elements and different forms of art, one can gain a deeper appreciation for the rich cultural traditions of Hinduism and the role that the elements play in shaping the natural world.

"Notice that the stiffest tree is most easily cracked, while the bamboo or willow survives by bending with the wind."

— Bruce Lee

ꕤ

XIV

The Five Elements and Hindu Environmentalism

The Five Elements, also known as the Pancha Mahabhutas in Hinduism, are the fundamental building blocks of the universe. These elements are Earth, Water, Fire, Air, and Space. They are believed to be the basic elements that make up all living and non-living things on Earth.

In Hinduism, the Five Elements are not only seen as a fundamental aspect of the natural world, but also as a spiritual concept. Each element is associated with certain qualities and characteristics, and it is believed that by understanding and harnessing the power of these elements, one can achieve balance and harmony in their own life.

One way in which the Five Elements are connected with Hindu environmentalism is through the concept of cleansing and purification. In Hindu rituals and practices, the elements are often used to purify the environment and create a sacred space. For example, fire is often used to burn incense or other offerings as a way of purifying the air and creating a positive energy. Water is also often used in rituals as a way of purifying the environment and purifying oneself.

In addition to these rituals, there are also various methods and practices connected with the Five Elements that can be used to clean and protect the environment. For example, the use of natural and biodegradable products can help to preserve the balance of the elements and protect the environment. Planting trees and other vegetation can also help to balance the elements and protect the environment, as they provide oxygen, absorb carbon dioxide, and help to regulate the climate.

Overall, the Five Elements and Hindu environmentalism are closely connected through the concept of cleansing and purification. By understanding and harnessing the power of these elements, Hindus believe that they can create a harmonious and balanced environment that is in tune with the natural world. Through the use of rituals, practices, and methods connected with the Five Elements, Hindus can work to protect and preserve the environment for future generations.

**“Breathing in, there is only the present moment.
Breathing out, it is a wonderful moment.”**

— Thich Nhat Hanh

XV

The Pancha Tatwa and the Gunas

The Pancha Tatwa, or Five Elements, and the Gunas are two important concepts in Hindu philosophy. The Five Elements are Earth, Water, Fire, Air, and Space, and they are believed to be the basic building blocks of the universe. The Gunas, on the other hand, are the three fundamental qualities or attributes that make up the universe. These Gunas are Satwik (Deva), Manushik (Manushya), and Rakshasik (Asur).

Each of the Five Elements is believed to be connected with one of the three Gunas. The element of Earth is associated with the Guna of Satwik, which represents purity, goodness, and spiritual evolution. The element of Water is associated with the Guna of Manushik, which represents the qualities of the human mind and emotions. The element of Fire is associated with the Guna of Rakshasik, which represents passion, desire, and the lower qualities of the ego.

The element of Air is believed to be a balance between the Gunas of Satwik and Manushik, representing both purity and the human mind. Finally, the element of Space is considered to be beyond the Gunas, representing the infinite and the absolute.

In Hindu philosophy, it is believed that the balance of the Gunas within an individual determines their state of mind and level of spiritual evolution. Those who are dominated by the Guna of Satwik are considered to be pure and spiritual, while those dominated by the Guna of Rakshasik are considered to be egoistic and materialistic. Those dominated by the Guna of Manushik are considered to be emotional and mental.

By understanding the connection between the Pancha Tatwa and the Gunas, one can gain a deeper understanding of the role that the Five Elements play in shaping the natural world and the qualities that make up the universe. This understanding can also help an individual to achieve balance and harmony within themselves and to pursue a path of spiritual evolution.

"That's life: starting over, one breath at a time."

— Sharon Salzberg

ꙮ

XVI

Begin and End with Pacha-Tatwa

By combining five elements, our body is formed and also merges into those five elements. When someone dies, we cremate his dead body in our Indian system| There are many other traditions in Indian science such as the tradition of flowing water, the tradition of making samadhi, etc. But it is usually burnt i.e. burnt. The tradition of cremation of dead bodies in India is especially prevalent in Hinduism.

After the removal of prana tattva from the body, the funeral rites of the dead person are performed, which is the last and important rites of the sixteen rites of Hinduism. This ritual is also called the last sacrifice. We see the dead person performing cremation at the crematorium, but thinking about the method of the last action, they only complete it| While you note that at that time the dead body gradually merges into the five elements.

Element of fire : When the body is burnt with fire, it merges into the fire element.

Sky element : The ether that is burned is found in the sky element.

Air elements : When smoke comes out, it gets mixed with the air element.

Soil elements : If the ash that falls on the earth after burning, it gets mixed with the soil element.

Water elements : When we immerse the bone in water, it gets mixed with the water element.

Other Books Of The Author

1. The Moments When I Met God
2. Kashiyile Theertha Pathangal
3. GURU GYAN VANI
4. Abhiprerak Gita
5. ASSI SE JAIN GHAT TAK
6. Hopelessness of Arjuna
7. The Soul and It's True Nature
8. Sense of Action (Karma)
9. Action through Wisdom
10. Action through Wisdom
11. THEORY AND PRACTICAL OF EVERY ACTION
12. LOGICAL UNDERSTANDING OF THE SUPREME
13. THE IMPERISHABLE SUPREME
14. Yatra Nishadraj se Hanuman Ghat Tak
15. Yatra Karnatak Ghat se Raja Ghat Tak
16. Yatra Pandey Ghat se Prayagraj Ghat Tak
17. Yatra Ranjendra Prasad Ghat se Dattatreya Ghat Tak
18. YaatraSindhiya Ghat se Gwaliar Ghat Tak
19. Yatra Mangala Gauri Ghat se Hanuman Gadhi Ghat Tak
20. Yatra Gaay Ghat Se Nishad Ghat Tak
21. MAA GANGA, GHATEN EVM UTSAV
22. Ganga Arti Dev Deepavali evam Any Utsav
23. Potentials of Digitalized India
24. VEDIC CONSCIOUSNESS
25. A Brief Introduction to Vedic Science
26. Kashi ke Barah Jyotirling
27. IMPACT OF MOTIVATION
28. Let's have a Milky Way Journey
29. Color Therapy in a Nutshell

30. Rigveda in a Nutshell
31. Yajurveda in a Nutshell
32. Samveda in a Nutshell
33. Atharva Veda in a Nutshell
34. Ayushman Bhava - Ayurveda
35. Srimad Bhagavad Gita and Upanishad Connection
36. Srimad Bhagavad Gita - an attempt to summarize each chapter.
37. Facts and Impact of Nakshatra
38. Astro Gems - NAVARATNA
39. Ekadashi - A Concise Overview
40. A Concise View of Hanuman Chalisa
41. Inspirational Gita
42. Nakshatraranyam
43. Summary of 18 Mahapuranas
44. Synopsis of 18 Upa Puranas
45. Rigvediya Upanishads
46. Shukla Yajurvediya Upanishads
47. Krishna Yajurvediya Upanishads
48. Samavediya Upanishads
49. Atharvavediya Upanishads
50. The Seven Great Sages
51. From Rocket Scientist to President Dr. APJ Abdul Kalam
52. The Visionary's Voice - Quotes of Dr. APJ Abdul Kalam
53. The Wisdom of Swami Vivekananda: Insights and Inspiration from a Legendary Spiritual Teacher
54. Ayurvedic Remedies from the Garden
55. Sages and Seers
56. Rising Strong – Motivational Stories of Women
57. Beyond Flames -Mystery stories of Funeral Ghat Manikarnika
58. The Origins of Tulsi: A Look at the Mythological Roots of the Plant"

59. "The Holistic Cow: A Look at the Physical, Spiritual, and Cultural Importance of Cows in India"
60. The Art of Healing - Art Therapy
61. Understanding the Five Elements: A Guide to Hindu Cosmology and Tradition"

Contact

DR. JAGADEESH PILLAI

PhD in Vedic Science

Four Times Guinness World Record Holder

Winner of Mahatma Gandhi Vishwa Shanti Puraskar and Global Peace Ambassador

Gemology, Astro & Vastu Consultant - Spiritual Counselor

Consultant for designing World Record Ideas

Efficient Tarot Card Reader

9839093003

myrichindia@gmail.com

drjagadeeshpillai@facebook

drjagadeeshpillai@instagram

jagadeeshpillai@youtube

www. JAGADEESHPILLAI.com

|| LOKAHA SAMASTHAHA SUKHINO BHAVANTU ||

www.ingramcontent.com/pod-product-compliance
Ingram Content Group UK Ltd.
Pitfield, Milton Keynes, MK11 3LW, UK
UKHW041958190726
13854UKWH00005B/2053

9 798889 354307